LOVE

UK

BELONG TO

....

....

....

I ♥ UK

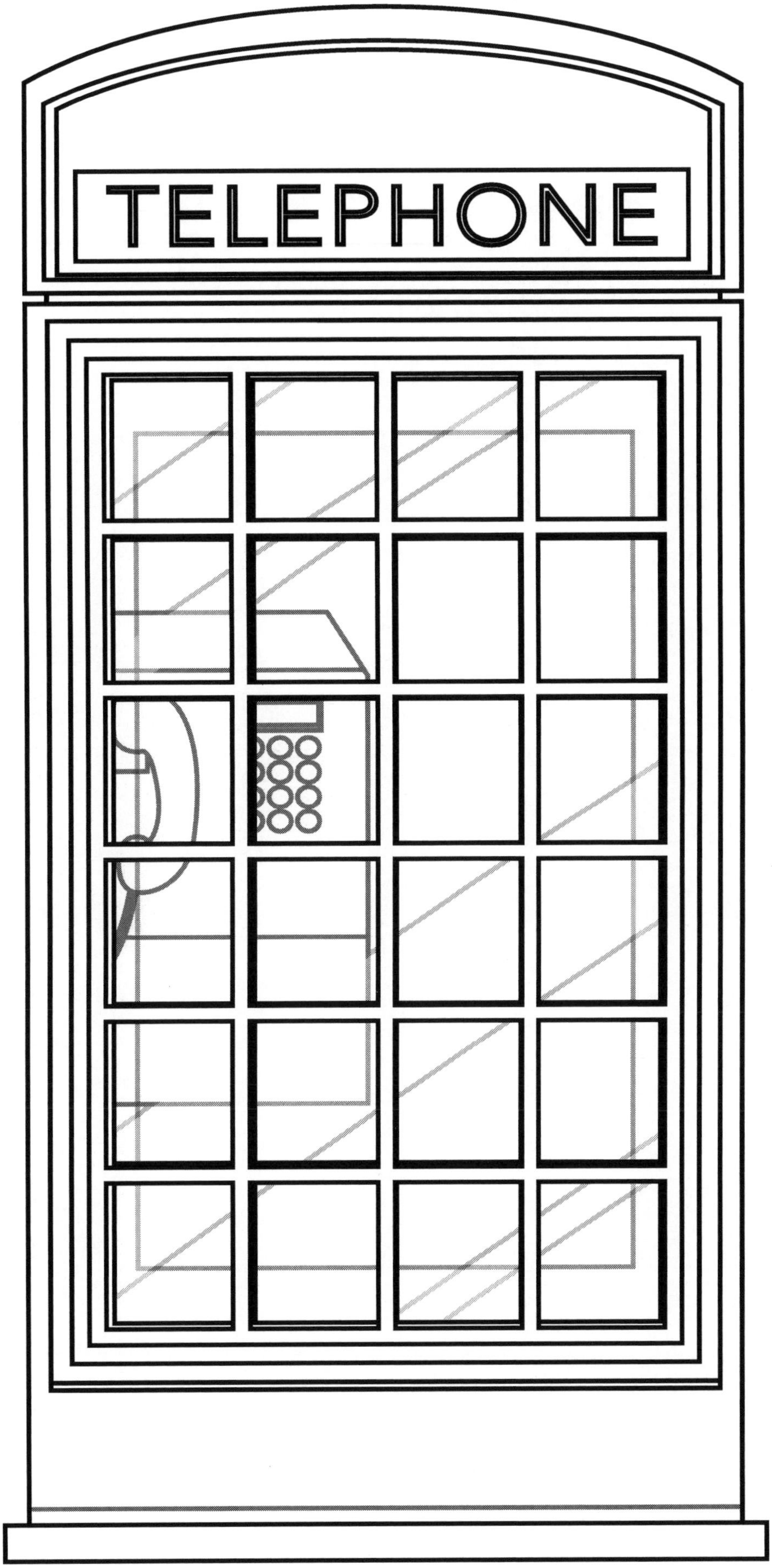
TELEPHONE

UK

I ♥ UK

LOVE
UK

i ♥
UK

LONDON
TELEPHONE

LONDON

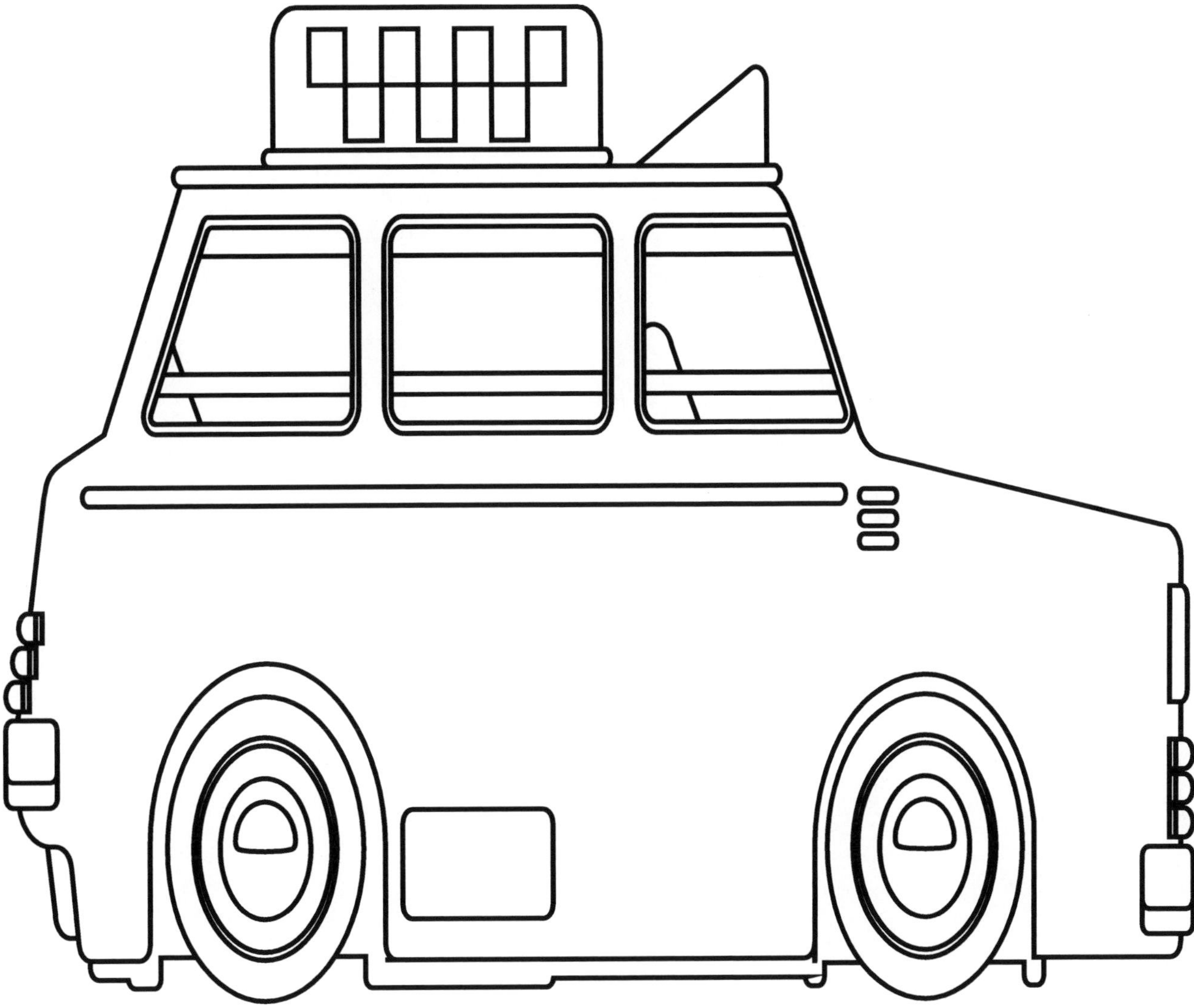

i
UK

TELEPHONE

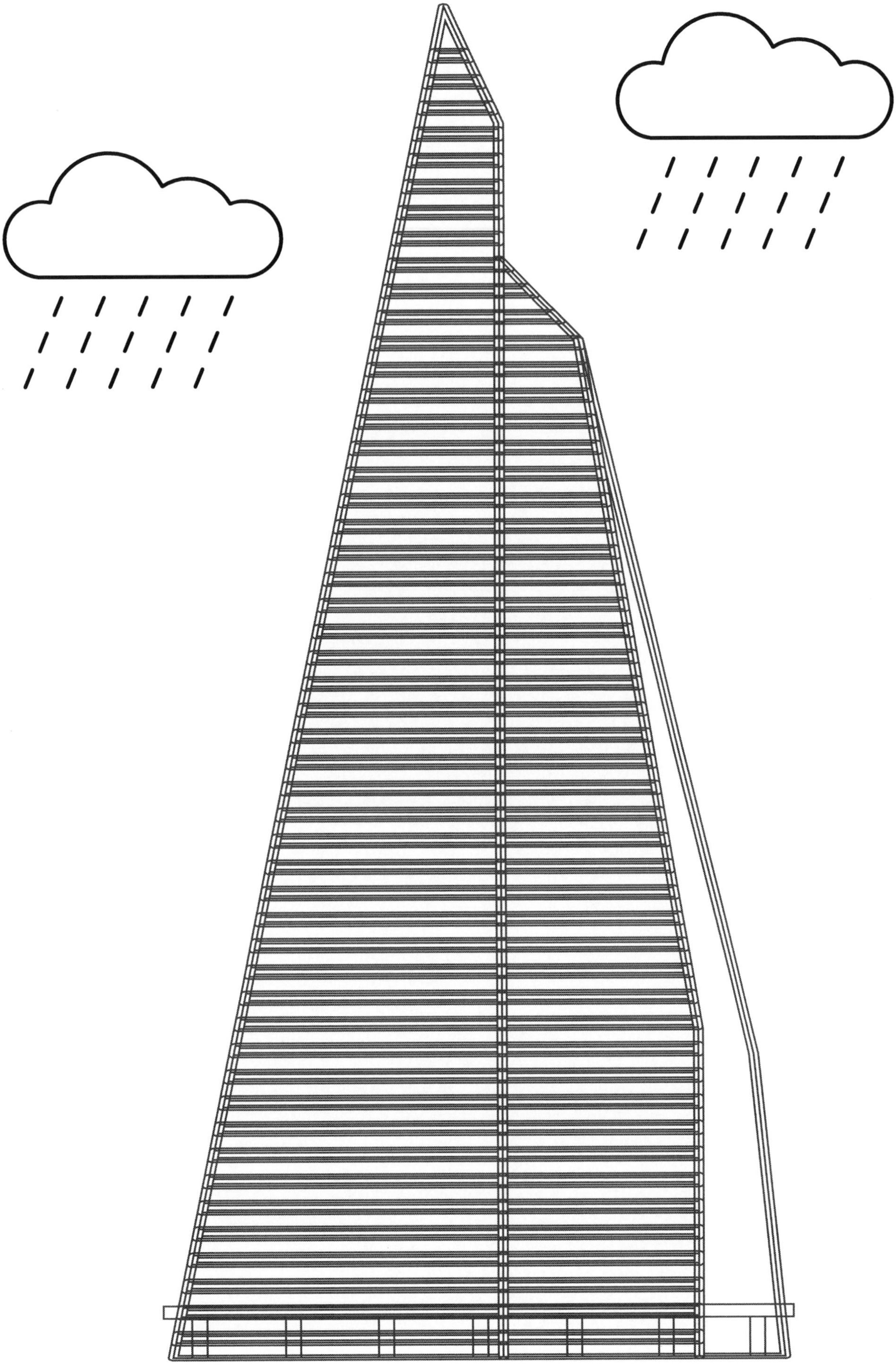

LONDON

TELEPHONE
LONDON

I
UK

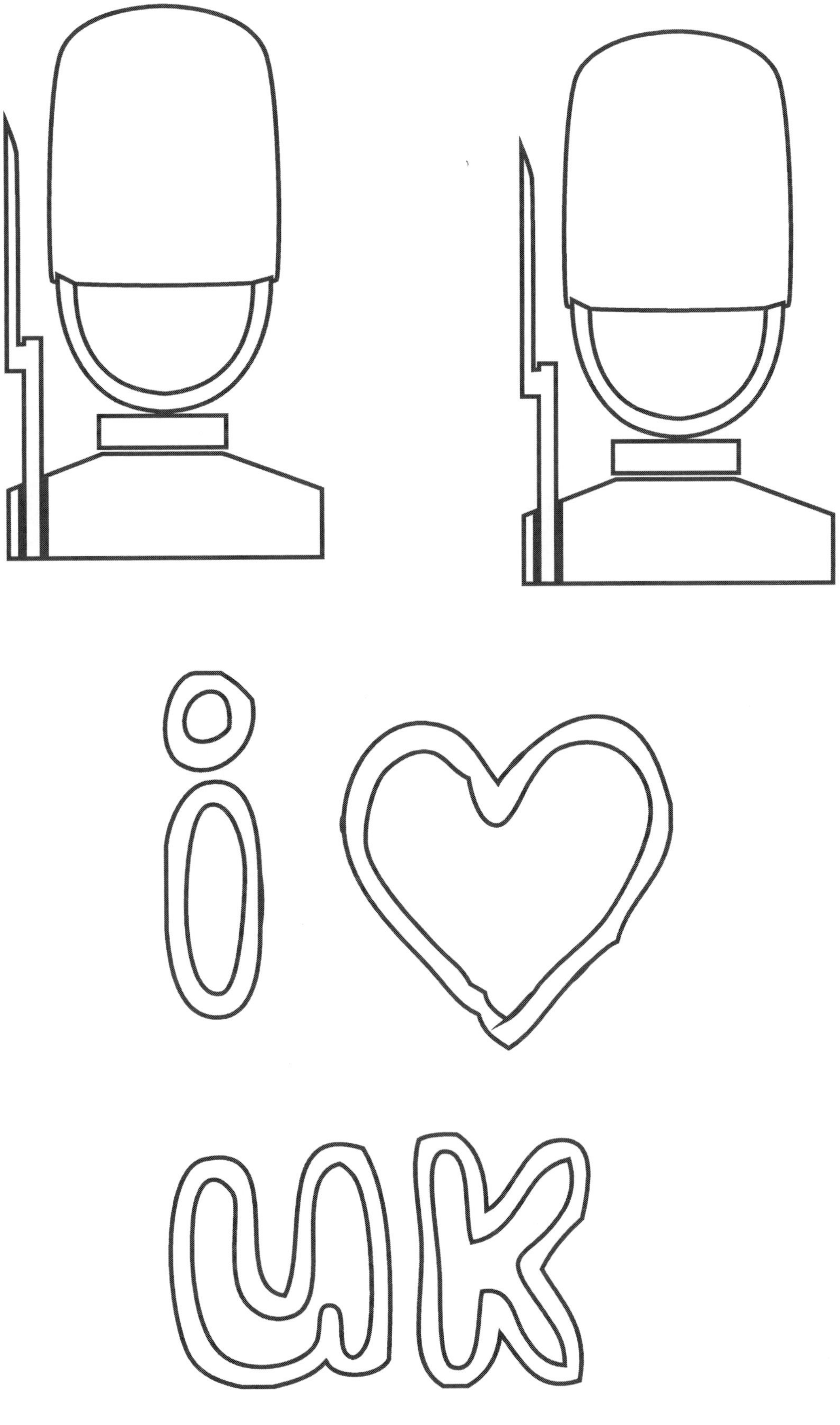
i ♥ uk

Please take a couple of minutes to leave us
a Review and Rating !!!

Thank you and good Luck !

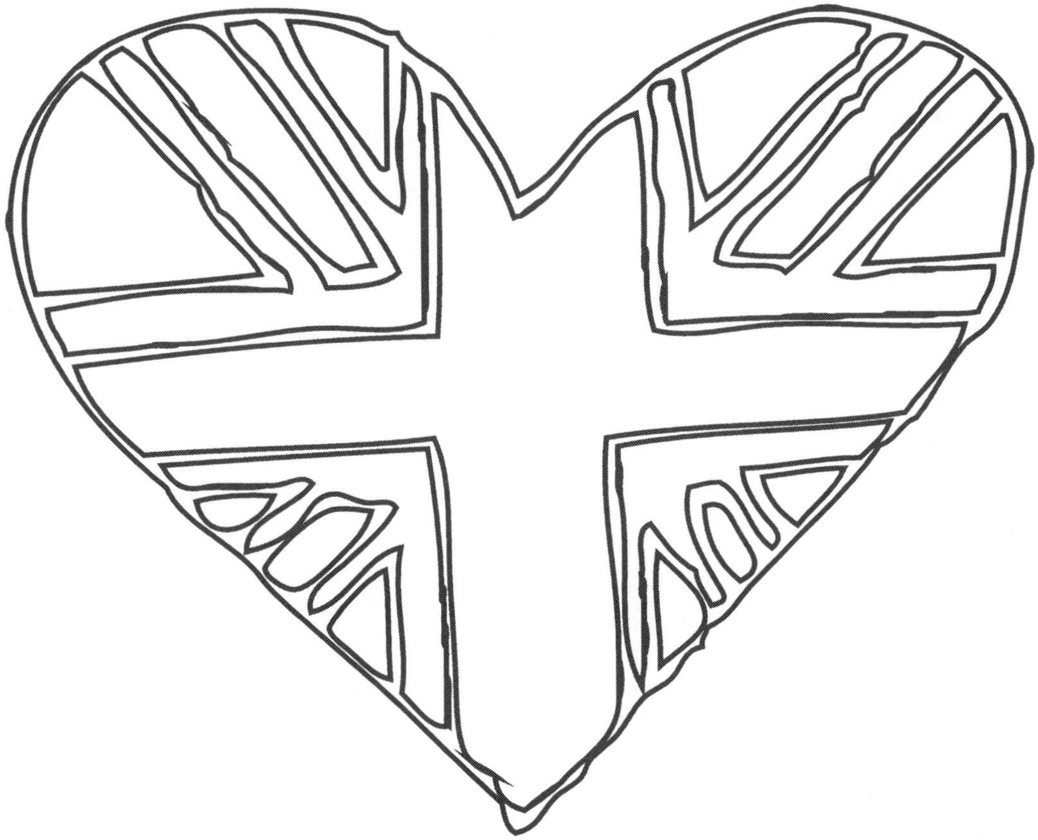

image credits to : vecteezy.com

Printed in Great Britain
by Amazon

63042891R00038